SCHOLASTIC

READ & RESPOND

Bringing the best books to life in the classroom

CW01560656

Activities based on Percy Jackson and the Lightning Thief

By Rick Riordan

Recommended system requirements:
Windows: XP (Service Pack 3), Vista (Service Pack 2), Windows 7 or Windows 8 with 2.33GHz processor
Mac: OS 10.6 to 10.8 with Intel Core™ Duo processor
1GB RAM (recommended)
1024 x 768 Screen resolution
CD-ROM drive (24x speed recommended)
Adobe Reader (version 9 recommended for Mac users)
Broadband internet connections (for installation and updates)

For all technical support queries (including no CD drive), please phone Scholastic Customer Services on 0845 6039091.

Designed using Adobe Indesign
Scholastic Education, an imprint of Scholastic Ltd
Book End, Range Road, Witney, Oxfordshire, OX29 0YD
Registered office: Westfield Road, Southam, Warwickshire CV47 0RA

Printed and bound by Ashford Colour Press
© 2016 Scholastic Ltd
1 2 3 4 5 6 7 8 9   6 7 8 9 0 1 2 3 4 5

British Library Cataloguing-in-Publication Data
A catalogue record for this book is available from the British Library.
ISBN 978-1407-16064-1

Author Sally Burt and Debbie Ridgard
Editorial team Rachel Morgan, Jenny Wilcox, Tracy Kewley and Becky Breuer
Series designer Neil Salt
Designer Anna Oliwa
Illustrator Moreno Chiacchiera/Beehive Illustration
Digital development Hannah Barnett, Phil Crothers and MWA Technologies Private Ltd
Acknowledgements
The publishers gratefully acknowledge permission to reproduce the following copyright material:

Penguin Random House UK for permission to use the cover and text from *Percy Jackson and the Lightning Thief* by Rick Riordan (Puffin Books 2005, 2013). Text copyright Rick Riordan, 2005.

Every effort has been made to trace copyright holders for the works reproduced in this book, and the publishers apologise for any inadvertent omissions.

CONTENTS ▼

Introduction   4

Using the CD-ROM   5

Curriculum links   6

About the book and author   8

Guided reading   9

Shared reading   13

Grammar, punctuation & spelling   19

Plot, character & setting   25

Talk about it   32

Get writing   38

Assessment   44

▼ INTRODUCTION

Read & Respond provides teaching ideas related to a specific children's book. The series focuses on best-loved books and brings you ways to use them to engage your class and enthuse them about reading.

The book is divided into different sections:

- **About the book and author:** gives you some background information about the book and the author.

- **Guided reading:** breaks the book down into sections and gives notes for using it with guided reading groups. A bookmark has been provided on page 12 containing comprehension questions. The children can be directed to refer to these as they read.

- **Shared reading:** provides extracts from the children's books with associated notes for focused work. There is also one non-fiction extract that relates to the children's book.

- **Grammar, punctuation & spelling:** provides word-level work related to the children's book so you can teach grammar, punctuation and spelling in context.

- **Plot, character & setting:** contains activity ideas focused on the plot, characters and the setting of the story.

- **Talk about it:** has speaking and listening activities related to the children's book. These activities may be based directly on the children's book or be broadly based on the themes and concepts of the story.

- **Get writing:** provides writing activities related to the children's book. These activities may be based directly on the children's book or be broadly based on the themes and concepts of the story.

- **Assessment:** contains short activities that will help you assess whether the children have understood concepts and curriculum objectives. They are designed to be informal activities to feed into your planning.

The activities follow the same format:

- **Objective:** the objective for the lesson. It will be based upon a curriculum objective, but will often be more specific to the focus being covered.

- **What you need:** a list of resources you need to teach the lesson, including digital resources (printable pages, interactive activities and media resources, see page 5).

- **What to do:** the activity notes.

- **Differentiation:** this is provided where specific and useful differentiation advice can be given to support and/or extend the learning in the activity. Differentiation by providing additional adult support has not been included as this will be at a teacher's discretion based upon specific children's needs and ability, as well as the availability of support.

The activities are numbered for reference within each section and should move through the text sequentially – so you can use the lesson while you are reading the book. Once you have read the book, most of the activities can be used in any order you wish.

Below are brief guidance notes for using the CD-ROM. For more detailed information, please click on the '?' button in the top right-hand corner of the screen.

The program contains the following:

- the extract pages from the book
- all of the photocopiable pages from the book
- additional printable pages
- interactive on-screen activities
- media resources.

Getting started

Put the CD-ROM into your CD-ROM drive. If you do not have a CD-ROM drive, phone Scholastic Customer Services on 0845 6039091.

- For Windows users, the install wizard should autorun, if it fails to do so then navigate to your CD-ROM drive. Then follow the installation process.
- For Mac users, copy the disk image file to your hard drive. After it has finished copying double click it to mount the disk image. Navigate to the mounted disk image and run the installer. After installation the disk image can be unmounted and the DMG can be deleted from the hard drive.
- To install on a network, see the ReadMe file located on the CD-ROM (navigate to your drive).

To complete the installation of the program you need to open the program and click 'Update' in the pop-up. Please note – this CD-ROM is web-enabled and the content will be downloaded from the internet to your hard drive to populate the CD-ROM with the relevant resources. This only needs to be done on first use, after this you will be able to use the CD-ROM without an internet connection. If at any point any content is updated, you will receive another pop-up upon start up when there is an internet connection.

Main menu

The main menu is the first screen that appears. Here you can access: terms and conditions, registration links, how to use the CD-ROM and credits. To access a specific book click on the relevant button (NB only titles installed will be available). You can filter by the

drop-down lists if you wish. You can search all resources by clicking 'Search' in the bottom left-hand corner. You can also log in and access favourites that you have bookmarked.

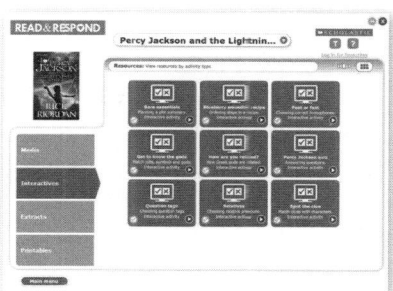

Resources

By clicking on a book on the Main menu, you are taken to the resources for that title. The resources are: Media, Interactives, Extracts and Printables. Select the category and then launch a resource by clicking the play button.

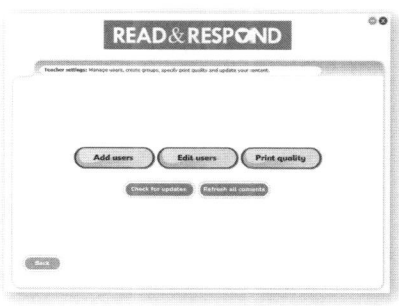

Teacher settings

In the top right-hand corner of the screen is a small 'T' icon. This is the teacher settings area. It is password protected, the password is: login. This area will allow you to choose the print quality settings for interactive activities ('Default' or 'Best') and also allow you to check for updates to the program or re-download all content to the disk via Refresh all content. You can also set up user logins so that you can save and access favourites. Once a user is set up, they can enter by clicking the login link underneath the 'T' and '?' buttons.

Search

You can access an all resources search by clicking the search button on the bottom left of the Main menu. You can search for activities by type (using the drop-down filter) or by keyword by typing into the box. You can then assign resources to your favourites area or launch them directly from the search area.

CURRICULUM LINKS

Section	Activity	Curriculum objectives
Guided reading		Comprehension: To check that the book makes sense to them, discussing their understanding and exploring the meaning of words in context.
Shared reading	1	Comprehension: To increase their familiarity with a wide range of books, including myths, legends and traditional stories, modern fiction, fiction from our literary heritage, and books from other cultures and traditions.
	2	Comprehension: To identify and discuss themes and conventions in and across a wide range of writing.
	3	Comprehension: To check that the book makes sense to them, discussing their understanding and exploring the meaning of words in context.
	4	Comprehension: To predict what might happen from details stated and implied.
Grammar, punctuation & spelling	1	Transcription: To use a thesaurus.
	2	Composition: To use a colon to introduce a list.
	3	Composition: To use expanded noun phrases to convey complicated information concisely.
	4	Composition: To use relative clauses.
	5	Composition: To differentiate between structures typical of informal and formal language.
	6	Transcription: To spell some words with 'silent' letters.
Plot, character & setting	1	Comprehension: To predict what might happen from details stated and implied.
	2	Comprehension: To explain and discuss their understanding of what they have read.
	3	Composition: To summarise the main ideas drawn from more than one paragraph.
	4	Comprehension: To identify and discuss conventions in and across writing.
	5	Comprehension: To discuss and evaluate how authors use language, considering the impact on the reader.
	6	Comprehension: To provide reasoned justifications for their views.
	7	Comprehension: To draw inferences such as inferring characters' feelings, thoughts and motives from their actions.
	8	Comprehension: To explain and discuss their understanding of what they have read.

Section	Activity	Curriculum objectives
Talk about it	1	Spoken language: To participate in debates.
	2	Spoken language: To participate in role play.
	3	Spoken language: To participate in presentations and performances.
	4	Spoken language: To participate in role play.
	5	Spoken language: To participate in discussion; to ask relevant questions to extend their understanding and knowledge.
	6	Spoken language: To give well-structured narratives.
Get writing	1	Composition: To use organisational and presentational devices to structure text and to guide the reader.
	2	Composition: To use organisational and presentational devices to structure text and to guide the reader.
	3	Composition: To select appropriate vocabulary; to use organisational devices to structure text.
	4	Composition: To describe settings, characters and atmosphere and integrate dialogue.
	5	Composition: To select appropriate grammar and vocabulary.
	6	Composition: To précis a longer passage.
Assessment	1	Spoken language: To participate in role play.
	2	Composition: To consider how authors develop characters.
	3	Transcription: To distinguish between homophones ; to use dictionaries to check the meaning of words.
	4	Comprehension: To understand what they read.
	5	Composition: To identify the audience for and purpose of the writing, selecting the appropriate form and models.
	6	Composition: To describe settings, characters and atmosphere.

PERCY JACKSON AND THE LIGHTNING THIEF

About the book

Percy Jackson and the Lightning Thief is the first book in a series of five entitled *Percy Jackson and the Olympians*. The stories are bursting with mythological characters and roller-coaster adventures as immortal gods collide with the mortal world. Twelve-year-old Percy has been to six schools in six years. Bad things just keep happening to him. Between that and his ADHD and dyslexia, Percy is convinced that what everyone says is true: he's a troubled kid. Everyone, that is, except his eccentric Latin teacher Mr Brunner, and Grover, his awkward best friend.

When Percy vaporises his maths teacher-cum-monster on a school outing, nothing will ever be the same again. Percy has to confront the heritage his mother has protected him from since birth: Percy is a half-blood – half boy, half god – and what's more, son of the sea god Poseidon. Equipped with a sword fit for the gods and a wry sense of humour, Percy accepts a quest to prevent war among the gods, but with a few plans of his own thrown in. As they set off across the US in search of the Underworld, Percy and his travelling companions are tested to the limit in true heroic fashion.

This is a witty, coming-of-age story, underpinned by serious issues and themes, from coming to terms with being different, to friendship, loyalty and tricky family relationships. An ideal novel to spark or extend children's interest in Ancient Greek mythology.

About the author

Born in San Antonio, United States, in 1964, Riordan was a middle school English and history teacher for 15 years. Having developed an early love of mythology, a love he furthered while teaching, he embarked on writing a series of adult mystery novels. Following the success of the *Tres Navarre* series, he began writing children's books. He was inspired by his son, recently diagnosed with ADHD and dyslexia, to invent new stories about the mythological world and, in 2005, Percy Jackson was born.

Riordan now writes full time and lives in Boston with his family. Riordan has also written other series based on mythology: the *Kane Chronicles*, the *Heroes of Olympus*, and *Magnus Chase*.

"It's not a bad thing to be different. Sometimes, it's the mark of being very, very talented. That's what Percy discovers about himself in *The Lightning Thief.*" *Rick Riordan*

Key facts

Percy Jackson and the Lightning Thief

Author: Rick Riordan

First published: 2005 by Miramax Books and later by Disney Hyperion.

Awards: The book has won many awards including the School Library Journal Best Book, Red House Children's Book Award and the CBBC Choice Award. It was a New York Times Bestseller and Notable Book of 2005.

Did you know: More than 45 million copies of Rick Riordan's books have been sold in more than 35 countries. In 2010, the book was adapted into a film and a graphic novel. *The Hidden Oracle*, the first in a series entitled *The Trials of Apollo*, was published in 2016. The series chronicles Apollo's adventures in New York, after Zeus casts him out of Olympus.

Getting ready to read

Read the title to the children. Ask: *What sort of book do you think this is? Why?* (fiction, fantasy, adventure: in real life people don't steal lightning) Find out if anyone has read other books in the series or seen the film. Read the blurb. Ask: *What does it tell you about the book?* (blurbs vary across editions but all reveal humour and an informal style; some show first-person narrative 'by Percy')

Review other items on the cover and preliminary pages – illustrations, author, publisher, reviews, awards – and discuss why publishers use these (to sell books; to persuade readers they will enjoy it). Finish by asking the children if think they will enjoy the book, and to give reasons.

Chapter 1: Introducing Percy

Read the first page in which Percy introduces himself. Ask: *What do you think a troubled kid is?* (discuss ADHD and dyslexia, and the challenges they present; be sensitive to children with similar issues) *Does Percy sound like a hero half-god?* (stereotypically, no) Read the remainder of the chapter and ask the children to recall the characters introduced (Percy, Mr Brunner, Grover, Nancy Bobofit, Mrs Dodds). Ask: *Which characters will be important? Why?* (Mr Brunner and Grover; Percy is positive about them) Point out how the outing allows the author to give background mythological information on Kronos and the Titan war. Ask: *Why does the author explain this part of Greek mythology?* (take predictions and later, refer back and link it to Percy's quest)

Chapters 2 to 4: Percy begins to discover his true identity

Ask the children to consider question 1 on the Guided Reading bookmark (page 12) while reading Chapters 2 to 4. Discuss the change in Percy after the museum trip (his grades plummet, he's crankier, has more fights and so on). Ask: *How would you feel if no one seemed to notice a teacher had disappeared?* (probably, like Percy, frustrated and confused)

In Chapter 3, focus on the descriptions of Sally Jackson and Gabe and what they imply. Ask the children to discuss question 18 on the bookmark. Explain that using physical appearance to indicate character is a literary device.

Ask: *How would you feel if your father left despite knowing about you?* (sad, angry, resentful; encourage empathy with Percy's feelings). Ascertain which mythological characters the children already know and list them, noting characters as they appear in the book. Read out the part in Chapter 4 when the minotaur ('bull-man') comes towards Percy. Invite the children to suggest adjectives to reflect the way Percy describes the monster (for example, humorous, unconventional, informal). Encourage them to think about question 15 on the bookmark.

Chapters 5 to 8: Son of the sea god

Ask the children to read Chapters 5 to 8 in groups. Note Percy's discoveries about mythology while at Camp Half-Blood (Mr Brunner being Chiron, the centaur, Mr D being Dionysus, and so on) and discuss question 4 on the Guided Reading bookmark.

After reading Chapter 6, ask: *What does 'undetermined' mean here?* (unclaimed by a god) At the end of Chapter 7, ask: *What clues indicate the identity of Percy's mother or father?* (Poseidon: Sally's love of the sea and meeting Percy's father there, the bathroom incident) Luke and Annabeth both refer to a quest. Ask: *What is a quest?* (a search for something, usually involving dangerous challenges)

Chapters 9 to 17: Percy's quest

Ask the children to think about questions 2 and 8 on the Guided Reading bookmark. Consider how quests parallel classic story structure: introduction, problem, build-up, climax, resolution, conclusion. Ask: *What does Percy's quest involve?* (finding Zeus's stolen bolt and returning it by summer solstice)

Together discuss question 16 on the bookmark (increasingly wild weather reflects growing anger of the gods) and then question 17 (Percy's dreams also provide insights into the immortal world; the eagle (Zeus) and horse (Poseidon) 'fighting' reflects their anger; later, the men fighting on the beach and saying 'Give it back' tells him something is missing; and the menacing voice of Kronos and the cavern imply darkness and evil). Ask: *Why does Zeus assume Percy stole the bolt?* (because Poseidon couldn't; Percy as his half-blood son could)

Point out wordplay as you go through (ambiguity, multiple meanings, implication, words in context, puns, idioms and expressions; for example, 'Wouldn't that put a twist in your toga?'). Read the Oracle's words (Chapter 9) aloud and discuss their meaning together and individually (for example, 'turned'). Return to the prophecy during the book to reflect on each part's meaning as the story unfolds. Ask the children to think about question 3 on the bookmark. Ask: *Why did Percy only tell Chiron the first two parts of the Oracle's prophecy?* (because he is concerned about betrayal and failing to save what matters most)

Together discuss questions 2 and 7 on the bookmark in relation to why Percy accepts the quest. (desire for revenge, to save his mother and fulfil the quest) Ask: *Are Percy's feelings those of a boy or a demigod/hero? What should his motivation be?* (Both. A hero looks at the bigger picture, whatever the personal cost. Encourage empathy for Percy's conflicted emotions.)

Point out Percy's dry, tongue-in-cheek comment on leaving the camp and discuss question 15 on the bookmark, noting Percy's use of humour to cope with something potentially unsettling or frightening. It is a recurrent technique the author employs to make darker aspects of the mythology more manageable, especially for children. Discuss how we often use humour to come to terms with difficult events or feelings.

Chapters 9 to 17 chart Percy and his companions' eventful journey to the Underworld. Reflect on question 5 from the bookmark as you read and consider the purpose of each episode; for example, Athena and Poseidon clashed over Medusa, whereas Percy and Annabeth must learn to work together and overcome their parents' rivalry. Discuss question 13 and encourage enjoyment of the modernised descriptions of mythological characters and places.

Chapters 18 to 22: Seeking resolution

Finally, the trio reach the Underworld. Before reading Chapter 18, remind the children that Charon ferries the dead across the River Styx to the Underworld, which is guarded by Cerberus, the three-headed dog. Bearing in mind both questions 13 and 15 on the Guided Reading bookmark, invite ideas about how the characters will be depicted.

Ask: *How does Hades' reaction to war differ from Percy's expectations?* (The Underworld is already overcrowded and congested, costing a fortune.) Ask: *What does this imply about Percy's assumptions about who stole the master bolt?* (that it was not Hades; his helmet was also stolen) By this time, sufficient clues indicate who/what is behind everything. Ask: *Who would benefit from a war of the gods?* (Kronos, imprisoned by Zeus for eternity, helped by Ares, jealous of the 'Big Three') At the end of Chapter 20, refer to the prophecy's final element. Ask: *What mattered most to Percy?* (His mother, but only to him; he saved his friends and himself to prevent war – and save the world – relying on Hades' honour to save his mother.) Ask: *Is Hades bad/evil?* (No, he does his job and keeps his word.)

After the Underworld climax, Percy seeks resolution. Ask: *What does Percy mean by 'settling his tab'?* (He must fulfil his quest and return the bolt, and Hades' helmet, to save his mother.) Ask: *How does Percy feel after meeting his father?* (He's glad of the distance, no surer of Poseidon than Poseidon is of Percy.) Together, discuss question 19 on the bookmark. Ask the children to predict what 'package' Poseidon has left for Percy. (Medusa's head) *What does Percy do with it?* (leaves it for his mother to find her own resolution)

When Percy returns to Camp Half-Blood, the prophecy remains unfulfilled. Ask the children to discuss question 20. Ask: *Why did Luke betray Percy?* (He is bitter, having failed his quest with no chance to redeem himself.) Together, discuss question 10. Although the prophecy is finally fulfilled, one issue remains unresolved: Kronos. Ask: *Why do you think nothing is done about Kronos stirring?* (opens the door to future adventures in later books)

Structure

Ask the children to think about question 11 on the Guided Reading bookmark. Focus on the chapter titles, encouraging enjoyment of each humorous summary. Using the contents page as a prompt, ask the children to organise the chapters into sections reflecting the story's progression (refer again to question 8).

- Chapters 1 to 4: Setting the scene – introducing Percy, his background, Camp Half-Blood.
- Chapters 5 to 17: Build-up – journey to the Underworld, quest challenges.
- Chapters 18 to 21: Climax and resolution – confronting Hades, challenging Ares, travelling to Olympus.
- Chapter 22: Conclusion: fulfilling the prophecy, returning.

Style

Ask the children to discuss question 12 on the Guided Reading bookmark and to come up with adjectives to describe Percy's narrative style (for example, humorous, informal, dry, witty, entertaining, sharp). Together, discuss question 9 on the bookmark. Encourage the children to notice Percy's asides in between recounting the action (for example, at the beginning of Chapter 6). Ask: *Why does the author use this technique?* (to give the reader background and insight into Percy's character, feelings and reactions) Ask: *How is this similar to an omniscient third person narrator?* (It allows the reader to learn things not directly related to the events in the story.)

Setting

Ask the children to think about question 14 on the Guided Reading bookmark. The story is punctuated by real places but these are paralleled by mythological places such as the Underworld and Mount Olympus which are accessed via real places. Talk about Olympus 'moving' throughout history to remain at the centre of Western civilisation. Ask: *Do you think America is the right place for Olympus?*

(This links to studies of religions, cultures and civilisations, as well as history and politics.)

Characters

As half god, half human, Percy spans both worlds, as does Annabeth. Grover and Chiron (Mr Brunner), however, are not gods: they are mythological characters. Help the children understand the characters and their significance by researching and learning about them in mythology (use both questions 13 and 18 on the Guided Reading bookmark). This will also help them to appreciate the humour of the modern settings and characterisation. Discuss questions 6 and 7 on the bookmark and help the children note Percy's transformation: how he becomes more confident and accepting of who he is, yet still loyal, funny and passionate.

Themes

The story, while on one level a rollicking adventure packed with larger-than-life characters and events, is at a deeper level a journey: Percy's coming-of-age journey. Refer to question 21 on the Guided Reading bookmark. While re-reading and reflecting on the novel, help the children to identify themes of friendship, loyalty, good versus evil, and what it means to be a 'hero' – both in traditional mythology and as Percy interprets it in the novel's modern setting. These themes are entwined with issues faced by many children: the nature of family, learning disabilities and feeling unlike others. Show the children how the book tackles difficult issues and makes them easier to deal with through humour and empathy.

■SCHOLASTIC
READ & RESPOND
Bringing the best books to life in the classroom

Percy Jackson and the Lightning Thief
By Rick Riordan

Focus on...
Meaning

1. What clues suggest Percy is different?

2. What does Percy's quest involve? Why does he do it?

3. Why does the prospect of his quest make Percy's emotions roll around 'like bits of glass in a kaleidoscope'?

4. How do Percy's perceptions of his 'learning difficulties' change at Camp Half-Blood?

5. What support do Annabeth and Grover give Percy in his quest?

6. How has Percy changed by the end of the book?

7. Discuss Percy's qualities both as a boy and as a hero.

Focus on...
Organisation

8. Which chapters fall into each stage of classic story structure?

9. How does Percy provide the reader with background information to the plot?

10. What indicates the book might be part of a series?

■SCHOLASTIC
READ & RESPOND
Bringing the best books to life in the classroom

Percy Jackson and the Lightning Thief
By Rick Riordan

Focus on...
Language and features

11. Why are the chapter titles significant?

12. How would you describe Percy's narrative style?

13. How does the author modernise mythological characters?

14. Are the settings in the book fact or fantasy?

15. How does the author use humour to manage frightening situations or characters?

Focus on...
Purpose, viewpoints and effects

16. How does weather create tension and reflect events in the immortal world?

17. How do Percy's dreams link to the story?

18. Do the characters' appearance reflect their personalities?

19. How do you think Percy felt about his father's prediction that a hero's fate is never happy?

20. Do you find Luke's actions understandable or forgivable?

21. What themes underpin the story? Which do you think is the most important?

Extract 1

- Share an enlarged copy of the extract with the children, marking it up as you read. Before starting, ask: *What do you notice about the paragraphs lengths?* (mostly short – one to two sentences – mirroring things flashing before him, as if actually happening)

- Read the whole extract. Encourage the children to listen, not follow, and to visualise the scene. Emphasise the descriptions and the sounds. Ask: *Which parts did you find especially evocative?* Re-read and highlight the parts that they mention, then point out other effects: echoing sounds – 'murk', 'lurched', 'swirled'; vivid imagery and comparisons – stepfather-sized catfish; graphic detail – 'soggy hamburger wrapper'; stimulating vocabulary – 'revelation', 'mortality', 'tumbled', 'trickling', 'quenched', 'sputtered' and so on. Underline the invented, onomatopoeic words, noting the colons to introduce and exclamation marks adding emphasis. Ask them to invent alternatives. Underline 'A whiteout of bubbles'. Ask: *What type of noun is 'whiteout' in this context?* (collective noun) Canvas other suggestions for collective nouns for bubbles.

- Focus on the writing techniques reflecting Percy's 'voice': short paragraphs, contrasting sentence length, verbless 'sentences', 'speaking style'. Ask: *How many sentences have no verb?* (four) *What effect do they have?* (add to the realism, reflecting his thinking in sudden bursts) Ask: *How are the paragraphs linked in the second half?* (a list of 'realizations' with specific pointing words: first, second, last) Underline the colons introducing ideas, used in a similar way to how the invented words were introduced.

- End with a reflection: *What would Grover have thought of the water Percy fell into? Why?* (He would have been horrified; Percy describes him as an environmentalist.)

Extract 2

- Prepare to read the extract in groups of three: narrator, Percy, Charon. Remind the children who Charon is and discuss their vision of him. Allow time for groups to annotate their parts, and discuss expression, emphasis and role play. Chat to groups as they prepare, collating points of interest on an enlarged copy.

- Focus on the details suggesting it is not an ordinary lobby: steel grey carpet and walls, 'skeleton' cactuses (note, not cacti), black couches, semi-transparent people. Ask: *Why was it called the 'DOA' lobby/recording studio?* (DOA is an initialism for 'dead on arrival'.)

- Ask: *Does Charon look how you expected? Why/why not?* (The children should realise Charon would be modernised, although later as he reaches the Underworld he morphs into the traditional ferryman on the Styx, no longer in an elevator.) Encourage the children to appreciate the detail employed to paint the picture and portray the characters – even to a black rose in Charon's lapel. Ask: *Why does Percy misread Charon's name tag?* (familiarity with Chiron combined with dyslexia)

- Focus on specific textual features: use of second person; present tense and punctuation related to conversation; unexpected juxtapositions – 'sweet and cold' smile; the simile; different sentence types and so on. Ask: *What effect do the capitals and italics create?* (different types of emphasis) *What suggests Percy is nervous?* (stammer: 'N-no.') Ask: *How do you think Percy felt at Charon's sarcasm and spelling out his name?* (possibly embarrassed or humiliated) Encourage empathy by thinking of situations in other contexts that could cause similar sentiments.

Extract 3

- Read the extract together, with you as the narrator and volunteers for the parts of Percy and Hades. While preparing, discuss how to interpret the text as a class. It's a conversation. Ask: *Which words indicate how to say the dialogue?* (Adverbs with 'said'; alternatives to 'said', such as 'bellowed', 'blurted'.) Point out that much of the dialogue has no explicit speaker. Ask: *What shows a change in speaker?* (new paragraph, with opening speech marks) Ask: *In the second paragraph, why are some of Percy's words italicised?* (indicates what he wanted to say, not what he said) *Why aren't speech marks used?* (he only thought the words)

- Initially, Percy feels intimidated by Hades' aura of power. What techniques make Hades seem less terrifying? (He's made more human, with regular, recognisable concerns; the humour in the ludicrous vision of Hades' concerns and the Underworld through his eyes offsets the darkness of the mythological version.) Ask: *Is Hades' reason for not wanting war what you expected?* (probably not)

- Ask: *What punctuation and text effects increase our understanding of the characters' feelings?* (italics for emphasis, exclamation marks, rhetorical questions, varied sentences types and lengths reflecting Hades' speech pattern, the ellipsis) Ask: *What does it mean here to be 'on a roll'?* (unstoppable, uninterruptable) *How would you describe the dialogue language? Give examples.* (informal: contractions, idiom, words ('guys', 'on a roll'), tone, sentence structure)

- End with a prediction: *What does Hades think Poseidon's plan is?*

Extract 4

- Provide each child with a copy of the extract and ask them to skim read the text. Ask: *Is the text fiction or non-fiction? What tells you this?* (non-fiction: columns, numbered headings) Ask: *Where would you find a text like this?* (encyclopaedia, reference book, internet and so on)

- Choose a reader for each paragraph. Ask the rest to follow, underlining unfamiliar words. Discuss any unfamiliar words at the end, highlighting them on an enlarged copy. Remind the children to use context as well as prior knowledge of word structure and origin.

- Paragraph one: Ask: *Why is 'dark' a good word in this context?* (multiple meanings: absence of light, evil, despair and so on) Ask: *What is the colon for?* (introduces a list)

- Paragraph two: Ask: *How is the list in the sentence 2 introduced?* (with an adverbial) Ask: *Which sentences begin with adverbials?* (sentence 2 – 'Following…'; sentence 4 – 'Although...') Underline 'perpetually', and ask: *What synonyms do you know for this word?* ('always', 'forever', 'eternally' and so on)

- Paragraph three: Ask: *What is the purpose of the dashes in sentence 2?* (to give additional information) *What else could you use?* (parenthesis: brackets or commas) *Can you find two pairs of antonyms? How are they linked?* ('idyll' and 'nightmare', 'good' and 'bad'; with 'nor') *What part of speech are the antonym pairs?* (two nouns, two adjectives)

- Ask: *What does the past tense suggest?* (that it no longer exists or is no longer believed) Ask: *Can you think of other questions that could be used as headings?* Collate the children's ideas to use later for research.

Extract 1

Chapter 14

I'd love to tell you I had some deep revelation on my way down, that I came to terms with my own mortality, laughed in the face of death, et cetera.

The truth? My only thought was: Aaaaggghhhhh!

The river raced towards me at the speed of a truck. Wind ripped the breath from my lungs. Steeples and skyscrapers and bridges tumbled in and out of my vision.

And then: *Flaaa-boooom!*

A whiteout of bubbles. I sank through the murk, sure that I was about to end up embedded in fifty metres of mud and lost forever.

But my impact with the water hadn't hurt. I was falling slowly now, bubbles trickling up through my fingers. I settled on the river bottom soundlessly. A catfish the size of my stepfather lurched away into the gloom. Clouds of silt and disgusting garbage – beer bottles, old shoes, plastic bags – swirled up all around me.

At that point I realized a few things: first, I had not been flattened into a pancake. I had not been barbecued. I couldn't even feel the Chimera poison boiling in my veins any more. I was alive, which was good.

Second realization: I wasn't wet. I mean, I could feel the coolness of the water. I could see where the fire on my clothes had been quenched. But when I touched my own shirt, it felt perfectly dry.

I looked at the garbage floating by and snatched an old cigarette lighter.

No way, I thought.

I flicked the lighter. It sparked. A tiny flame appeared, right there at the bottom of the Mississippi.

I grabbed a soggy hamburger wrapper out of the current and immediately the paper turned dry. I lit it with no problem. As soon as I let it go, the flames sputtered out. The wrapper turned back into a slimy rag. Weird.

But the strangest thought occurred to me only last: I was breathing. I was underwater, and I was breathing normally.

Extract 2

Chapter 18

We walked inside the DOA lobby.

Muzak played softly on hidden speakers. The carpet and walls with steel grey. Pencil cactuses grew in the corners like skeleton hands. The furniture was black leather, and every seat was taken. There were people sitting on couches, people standing up, people staring out the windows or waiting for the elevator. Nobody moved, or talked, or did much of anything. Out of the corner of my eye, I could see them all just fine, but if I focused on any one of them in particular, they started looking … transparent. I could see right through their bodies.

The security guard's desk was a raised podium, so we had to look up at him.

He was tall and elegant, with chocolate-coloured skin and bleached-blonde hair shaved military style. He wore tortoiseshell shades and a silk Italian suit that matched his hair. A black rose was pinned to his lapel under a silver name tag.

I read the name tag, then looked at him in bewilderment. 'Your name is Chiron?'

He leaned across the desk. I couldn't see anything in his glasses except my own reflection, but his smile was sweet and cold, like a python's, right before it eats you.

'What a precious young lad.' He had a strange accent – British, maybe, but also as if he had learned English as a second language. 'Tell me, mate, do I look like a centaur?'

'N-no.'

'Sir,' he added smoothly.

'Sir,' I said.

He pinched the name tag and ran his finger under the letters. 'Can you read this, mate? It says C-H-*A*-R-O-N. Say it with me: CARE-ON.'

'Charon.'

'Amazing! Now: *Mr* Charon.'

'Mr Charon,' I said.

'Well done.' He sat back. "I *hate* being confused with that old horse-man. And now, how may I help you little dead ones?'

Extract 3

Chapter 19

Hades bellowed, 'Do you think I *want* war, godling?'

I wanted to say, *Well, these guys don't look like peace activists.* But I thought that might be a dangerous answer.

'You are Lord of the Dead,' I said carefully. 'A war would expand your kingdom, right?'

'A typical thing for my brothers to say! Do you think I need more subjects? Did you not see the sprawl of Asphodel?'

'Well…'

'Have you any idea how much my kingdom has swollen in this past century alone, how many subdivisions I've had to open?'

I opened my mouth to respond, but Hades was on a roll now.

'More security ghouls,' he moaned. 'Traffic problems at the judgment pavilion. Double overtime for the staff. I used to be a rich god, Percy Jackson. I control all the precious metals under the earth. But my expenses!'

'Charon wants a pay rise,' I blurted, just remembering the fact. As soon as I said it, I wished I could sew up my mouth.

'Don't get me started on Charon!' Hades yelled. 'He's been impossible ever since he discovered Italian suits! Problems everywhere and I've got to handle all of them personally. The commute time alone from the palace to the gates is enough to drive me insane! And the dead just keep arriving. *No*, godling. I need no help getting subjects! *I did not ask for this war.*'

'But you took Zeus's master bolt.'

'Lies!' More rumbling. Hades rose from his throne, towering to the height of a football goalpost. 'Your father may fool Zeus, boy, but I am not so stupid. I see his plan.'

'His plan?'

Extract 4

The Ancient Greek Underworld

Where was the Underworld?

In Ancient Greek mythology, the Underworld was believed to be a dark place, deep beneath the earth, where the souls of the dead were believed to go. Geographically, most depictions show it to be bounded by five great rivers: Styx (unbreakable oath), Acheron (woe), Cocytus (lamentation), the Phlegethon (fire) and Lethe (forgetfulness).

Who ruled the Underworld?

The Underworld was sometimes known as Hades, after the god who ruled it. Following Zeus's overthrow of his father, Kronos, and the Titans, he and his Olympian brothers, Poseidon and Hades, divided the world into kingdoms with Zeus ruling the sky, Poseidon the sea and Hades the Underworld. Hades was believed to be perpetually seeking to swell the number of souls in his realm. Although all were granted entry to the Underworld, Cerberus, the three-headed dog guarding the gate, allowed none to leave.

What happened to the dead souls?

According to mythology, Hermes escorted the souls of the dead to the Underworld entrance. Charon then ferried those who could pay across the river – family or friends would leave a coin in a dead person's mouth – leaving the rest to wander eternally trapped betwixt two worlds. On arrival, all souls were judged according to their deeds when alive by a panel of three mortals: the select few judged to have led virtuous lives were destined for the idyllic Elysian fields, the Furies escorted the wicked down to the horrors of Tartarus, with the Plain of Asphodel, a shadowy, desolate place neither idyll nor nightmare, for those judged neither good nor bad.

GRAMMAR, PUNCTUATION & SPELLING

1. A treasure chest of words

Objective

To use a thesaurus.

What you need

Copies of *Percy Jackson and the Lightning Thief*, photocopiable page 22 'Word analysis', printable page 'Open the treasure chest', thesauruses, dictionaries.

What to do

- Rick Riordan uses an exciting range of vocabulary throughout the novel: formal and informal, evocative and ordinary. Check that the children fully understand 'evocative' and the difference between formal and informal.

- Hand out copies of photocopiable page 22 'Word analysis'. Choose a page in the book and call out words asking the children in which quadrant they would place the word. For example, from the opening paragraphs of Chapter 4: 'dark' – ordinary, formal; 'mom' – informal, ordinary, 'flitted' – evocative, formal.

- Work in groups to complete the photocopiable sheet. Either select a page or let the groups choose. Challenge the children to find at least one word to write in each quadrant, preferably more.

- Ask: *What do you look for in a dictionary and a thesaurus?* (definitions; synonyms and antonyms) Ask the groups to complete printable page 'Open the treasure chest', using some of the words from the 'Word analysis' activity. The children will not only learn or reinforce meanings, but will find synonyms to help them appreciate nuance and shades of meaning. Ask: *Are all the synonyms interchangeable?* (not always – not all synonyms fit in the context; it takes experience and judgment to know)

Differentiation

Support: Write words from a particular page on the sheet for selected groups to look up, taking away the difficulty of choosing.

2. Listing matters

Objective

To use a colon to introduce a list.

What you need

Extracts 1 and 4, notebooks, photocopiable page 23 'Using colons to list'.

What to do

- Begin with a warm-up activity. Call out the names of various Ancient Greek gods and goddesses for the children to write in their notebooks; for example, Zeus, Poseidon, Chiron, Hades, Hermes, Ares, Athena and so on. (It could also be a spelling activity.) At the end, ask: *How did you write the words? One per line or along the line?* (a list) *Why?*

- Ask: *How are lists presented and punctuated in written texts?* (along the line, separated by commas or semi-colons, or as bullets) Ask: *How are lists usually introduced in texts?* (with a colon or sometimes with words such as 'for example')

- Ask pairs to find examples of lists in Extracts 1 and 4 and highlight them, noting how they are introduced and punctuated. Discuss the differences.

- Ask: *How else are colons used in Extract 1?* (to introduce a particular word for emphasis) Ask: *Can you think of other things a colon can introduce?* (dialogue in plays and so on)

- Briefly go over photocopiable page 23 'Using colons to list' and then allow the class to work through it independently.

Differentiation

Support: Work through the first part of the photocopiable page with those needing more support and then monitor progress.
Extension: Encourage anyone who has finished to invent additional list scenarios for a partner to complete.

3. Nifty noun phrases

Objective

To use expanded noun phrases.

What you need

Notebooks, slips of paper.

What to do

- Revise phrases: groups of words working together, without a verb. Ask: *What is an adjective/adverb/ noun phrase?* (a group of words acting as a single adjective/adverb/noun)

- Play an oral speed game to revise noun phrases. Go round the class: you say a noun; they say an adjective to go with it. Choose one to work through, and remind them that the articles (the/a/ an) are part of the phrase. Gradually add adjectives (separated by commas) demonstrating how the mind picture develops. For example, 'The silver sword is mine' becomes 'The ancient, bejewelled razor-edged sword is mine'.

- Expanded noun phrases modify nouns quickly and efficiently, and incorporate articles, adjectives and/or phrases. Work through the following phrase (from Chapter 4) on the board: 'a huge, White House Christmas-tree-sized pine at the crest of the nearest hill'. Ask: *Which noun is modified?* (pine) *What does the phrase tell you about the pine tree?* (size and location in precise detail) Demonstrate how the words work together forming an overall phrase to expand the visual image.

- Write a selection of words on the board and ask groups to write expanded noun phrases on slips of paper; for example, 'monster', 'sword', 'hero', 'river'. Share the phrases.

Differentiation

Support: Provide children with a word bank to use as a resource, including both words and phrases.
Extension: Encourage children to be adventurous with complex structures, combining multiple adjectives/phrases.

4. Relatives add value

Objective

To use relative clauses.

What you need

Photocopiable page 24 'Relative matters', interactive activity 'Relatives'.

What to do

- Relative clauses are dependent (subordinate) clauses, introduced by a relative pronoun (commonly 'who', 'whom', 'whose', 'which', 'that', 'where', 'when', or an implied one). They usually add detail to a noun, or help writing flow by joining sentences. The extra detail comes after the noun and is usually set off in commas.

- Point out when 'that' is used to clarify the noun, it has no commas, or the relative pronoun can be omitted.

- Write on the board: 'Mr Brenner is my Latin teacher. Mr Brenner is a centaur.' Ask: *How can you use 'who' to join the sentences in two ways?* ('Mr Brenner, who is my Latin teacher, is a centaur.' or 'Mr Brenner, who is a centaur, is my Latin teacher.') Write both on the board. Underline the relative clause, highlighting the pronoun. Ask: *Which is the head noun?* (Mr Brenner) *What type of relative clause is it?* (non-defining, set off by commas)

- Use the interactive activity 'Relatives' to practise, while also explaining the various pronoun roles ('who' for people; 'which' or 'that' for animals or things; 'whose' for possession; 'when' and 'where' for relative time and place)

- Hand out photocopiable page 24 'Relative matters' for the children to work on in pairs before sharing answers as a class.

Differentiation

Support: Ask children to complete only the first activity, where they choose a relative pronoun.
Extension: Children can expand their knowledge of relative clauses by identifying them in *Percy Jackson and the Lightening Thief*.

5. Informally formal

Objective

To differentiate between structures typical of informal and formal language.

What you need

Copies of *Percy Jackson and the Lightning Thief*, interactive activity 'Question tags'.

What to do

- Ask: *When do we use formal and informal language?* (formal – most writing, speaking formally; informal – conversation, emails, texts) Discuss narrative and dialogue in fiction. Usually, narrative is formal and dialogue less so – authors use different choices of grammar and vocabulary.

- Read aloud the first section of Chapter 1. Ask: *Is it narrative or dialogue?* (narrative) *Does it sound formal or informal? Why?* (informal; choice of first person, reader directly 'addressed', informal sentence structures, words, contractions and so on)

- Explain that we often use question tags when speaking informally. Open the interactive activity 'Question tags' and work through the first two screens together. Explain that each statement's auxiliary verb (or verb 'to be') is echoed by the tag verb. The statement subject is the same as the tag subject. Positive statements usually have negative tags and vice-versa. Ask the children for examples and check if they follow these rules. Ask: *Why do we use them?* (to confirm something or to encourage a response) Point out that single words sometimes perform the same function: 'OK?', 'Right?', 'Yeah?' and so on.

- Ask the children to complete the rest of the interactive activity independently.

Differentiation

Extension: Ask children to skim through *Percy Jackson and the Lightning Thief* for question tag examples.

6. Listen for the 'silents'

Objective

To spell some words with 'silent' letters.

What you need

Copies of *Percy Jackson and the Lightning Thief*, printable page 'Silent bingo', dictionaries.

What to do

- Silent letters can be a challenging aspect of English spelling. Remind the children that much of English spelling stems the words' roots in Latin, Greek, French, German, Old English and so on (like inheriting features from parents).

- Challenge teams to list words containing silent letters in a timed period, skimming through *Percy Jackson and the Lightning Thief* to help them. At the end, teams score a point for each silent letter word no other team has.

- Classify their words on the board by silent letter; for example, 'b', 'w', 'k', 't', 'g', 'l', 'c', 'p', 'u'. Discuss where in the words the silent letters appear to increase awareness of letter patterns. For example: at the beginning, 'p – psalm', 'k – knee', 'w – wrong', 'g – gnome'; in the middle, 'l – walk', 't – whistle', 'g – sign', 'u – biscuit'; or at the end, 'n – hymn', 'b – comb'.

- Cut out the bingo cards from printable page 'Silent bingo' and call out a silent letter. If a child can think of a word with that silent letter, they write it down and cross the letter off the card. The first one to complete a card with correctly spelled words wins that round. Encourage them to use dictionaries to check their words.

Differentiation

Support: Let children work in pairs or small groups for the bingo.

Word analysis

- Choose eight words from *Percy Jackson and the Lightning Thief* and write them down with their page numbers.
- Write the part of speech for each word.
- Then decide how to classify each word: formal or informal, and ordinary or evocative. Write each word into the correct quadrant (square) on the grid at the bottom.

Page	Chosen word	Part of speech

	Formal	Informal
Ordinary		
Evocative		

Using colons to list

● Order each set of words into a sentence with a list. Then add the colon and any other necessary punctuation. The first and last words in each set are in the correct place.

Olympus and the United France Spain England has been in Greece many places located Germany States.

_____

_____

Percy half boy he was chatting to mythical characters realised he was not ADHD many things he understood he really was Ancient Greek and half god.

_____

_____

● Rewrite each bulleted list as a sentence which includes the list. Add a sensible introduction, colon and correct punctuation.

● blue candy
● blue corn tortillas
● blueberry smoothies
● blue birthday cakes

● he would go to the Underworld
● he would rescue his mother
● he would return the master bolt
● he would meet his father

1. _____

_____

_____

_____

_____

2. _____

_____

_____

_____

_____

Relative matters

● Choose one of the pronouns to fill each space.

---

who, whom, whose, which, that, where, when

Percy, _____ father is Poseidon, is a half-blood.

The camp, _____ is for demigods, should be safe for Percy.

Grover was someone _____ loyalty Percy never questioned.

The person _____ betrayed Percy was from Camp Half-Blood.

The school _____ Percy attended this year is in New York.

● Combine sentence pairs by changing the second sentence into a relative clause using a relative pronoun or an implied one.

The naiad gave Percy the three pearls. They saved his life.

_____

Percy met Mr D. Mr D was really the god Dionysus.

_____

Percy was curious about the prophecy. The prophecy was revealed by the Oracle.

_____

Olympus is the gods' home. The gods are named after it.

_____

Luke went on a disappointing quest. Luke's father is Hermes.

_____

PLOT, CHARACTER & SETTING

1. Looking back at where it all began

Objective

To predict what might happen from details stated and implied.

What you need

Copies of *Percy Jackson and the Lightning Thief*, photocopiable page 29 'Clue log', etymological dictionary (available online).

Cross-curricular link

History

What to do

- Re-read the first section of Chapter 1. Ask: *When in the story is this section set? How can you tell?* (sometime after the end of the main story; Percy is telling people what might happen as they read it) Demonstrate the word origin of 'prologue', using an etymological dictionary if possible. Ask: *Where did the word originate?* (Ancient Greek: 'pro', before; 'logos', speaking) Prologues, originally used in Greek plays, are separate from the plot, and provide background or foreshadow later events. Ask: *What does this prologue suggest about the story to come?* (involves half-bloods, danger, a threat and that all may not be what it seems) *Who do you think 'they' might be?* (possibly characters from Greek mythology)

- Hand out photocopiable page 29 for the children to start a log of clues to future events throughout the book. To begin, ask them to re-read Chapter 1, noting any clues to back their prologue ideas or predictions of later events. Ask: *Why did the author choose the Kronos story?* (it will be relevant later; it ensures the reader knows the mythology)

Differentiation

Support: Assign children a 'clue buddy' to share their log and ideas with.

Extension: Ask for volunteers at the end of sessions to present their clues and ideas to the class.

2. All for one, one for all

Objective

To explain and discuss their understanding of what they have read by drawing up character profiles.

What you need

Copies of *Percy Jackson and the Lightning Thief*, A1 or A2 card, scissors, glue, art supplies.

Cross-curricular links

History, art and design

What to do

- Percy, Annabeth and Grover complement each other. Each character's skills are needed for Percy to succeed in his quest. Divide the class into groups and assign each a character to discuss. Ask: *What words or phrases describe your character?* After a few minutes, each group should choose a spokesperson to present their group's ideas to the class. Now ask: *What are your character's distinctive attributes, characteristics or gifts?* Explain that each aspect must be supported by evidence from the book. For example, Grover's affinity with the environment is shown by his desire to find Pan and eating discarded tin cans; Percy's affinity with water is shown when he conjures up a giant wave and breathes underwater.

- Walk around exchanging views and making suggestions before bringing the class together to share ideas. Discuss how challenging characteristics in one context may be advantageous in another; for example, Percy was diagnosed with ADHD in school but this turned to his advantage when sword fighting. Establish whether any characteristics are shared by all (for example, loyalty).

- Ask each group to design a profile board on A1 or A2 card for the wall, using words, phrases, images, expressions and so on. These can also be added to over time.

▼ PLOT, CHARACTER & SETTING

3. Parallel realities

Objective
To summarise the main ideas drawn from more than one paragraph.

What you need
Copies of *Percy Jackson and the Lightning Thief*, media resource 'Map of Long Island', atlases or online maps, printable page 'Map of the USA'.

Cross-curricular link
Geography

What to do

- Begin by asking: *What is the opening setting for the novel?* (in and around New York, USA) Ask the children to re-read Chapter 5, where Grover escorts Percy to Chiron and Mr D. Ask: *What is a 'Sound' in this context?* (a large ocean inlet or deep bay) Show the media resource 'Map of Long Island' and ask a volunteer to point out the Sound, Montauk and the possible whereabouts of Camp Half-Blood. Ask: *Is Camp Half-Blood a real location?* (no, fantasy but situated in/accessed from a real location) Ask: *What other fantasy places are accessed via real locations?* (the Underworld and Olympus)

- Provide printable page 'Map of the USA' and ask the children to find some of the real locations mentioned in the book in an atlas or online map. Then ask to them mark each place the trio had a fantastical encounter using a symbol (for example, a lotus flower for the Lotus Hotel). Ask them to create a key on a separate sheet, briefly summarising each encounter, including: place name, specific location (for example, Empire State Building), date, who was encountered, what happened and, if possible, who the character is in mythology.

- Choose one of the keys to read out.

Differentiation
Extension: Encourage children to include the trio's modes of transport and other landmarks in their keys.

4. The hero's journey

Objective
To identify and discuss conventions in and across writing.

What you need
Photocopiable page 30 'Percy's heroic journey', media resource 'The heroic journey'.

Cross-curricular link
History

What to do

- Briefly revise the phases of classic story structure: introduction, problem, build-up, climax, resolution, conclusion. Ask: *How does this story follow this pattern?* (Percy discovers he is a half-blood; Zeus's master bolt is stolen, potential for war; Percy's quest, ordeals on his journey; the climax as Percy battles Ares; returning the bolt, saving his mother; finally, coming to terms with his heritage.)

- Introduce the 'heroic journey' concept: the story pattern found in ancient myths and many modern 'hero' adventures. Use the media resource 'The heroic journey' to show the stages: ordinary world; call to adventure; refusal of call/quest; supernatural aid; crossing the threshold to 'special world'; tests, allies and enemies; approach; ordeal; reward, journey home; atonement; return (or presented in key phases: Call, Test, Transformation, Return). Ask: *Is Percy's journey a heroic journey?* (yes)

- Hand out photocopiable page 30 'Percy's heroic journey'. Ask the children to read the stage summaries and compare them to the contents page in the book. Ask volunteers to suggest which chapters fall into each stage and discuss as a class before the children complete the sheet.

Differentiation
Support: Children can omit the reasons column.
Extension: Challenge children to find other myths ('Odysseus', 'Labours of Hercules') or modern-day books/films following a similar pattern (Disney's *Hercules* and *Lilo & Stitch*).

5. Language matters

Objective

To discuss and evaluate how authors use language, considering the impact on the reader.

What you need

Copies of *Percy Jackson and the Lightning Thief*, notebooks.

What to do

- Read out Percy's encounter with the minotaur in Chapter 4 from 'I looked back'. Ask: *What atmosphere is created when Percy first sees the minotaur?* (fear, tension, panic) *What words and images create this effect?* (For example, 'skin crawl', 'swallowed hard', 'flash of lightning', 'Run and don't look back', 'shouted', 'moaned'.) *How does Percy describe the minotaur as he glances back?* ('seven feet tall' and so on.) Discuss how the author counterbalances Percy's fear with his humorous, adolescent, dry wit, which is almost mocking and often sarcastic.

- Explain that pairs are going to describe the minotaur in a formal, third-person narrative paragraph (no similes or slang like 'ceps', meaning biceps). Allow five to ten minutes to skim for information then ask the pairs to write their descriptive paragraph in their notebooks. Remind them that information should be gleaned from several paragraphs.

- Invite pairs to read out their descriptions. Build a consensus profile on the board focusing on word choice, sentence structure and style. Ask: *Would the novel be as enjoyable if it had a more formal third person narrator? Why?* (possibly not; the first person narrative and Percy's style make it easier to associate with him)

Differentiation

Support: Offer a starter sentence for the writing: 'The monster was seven feet tall, with immense biceps and triceps.'
Extension: Ask the children to rewrite another 'Percy-style' description of a person or scene.

6. Son of Poseidon stand up

Objective

To provide reasoned justifications for their views.

What you need

Copies of *Percy Jackson and the Lightning Thief*, photocopiable page 31 'Clues and predictions', interactive activity 'Spot the clue'.

What to do

- Ask: *Which Olympian god is Percy's father? When did Percy find out?* (Poseidon; after the hellhound attack) Ask: *Do you think Percy suspected Poseidon was his father? Why?* (If Percy suspected, he didn't share his suspicions with the reader.)

- Remind the children that Percy is writing 'after the event'. He does, however, foreshadow or give clues about later revelations and events; for example, at the end of Chapter 7, he states 'I wish I'd known how briefly I would get to enjoy my new home'.

- Use interactive activity 'Spot the clue' and then demonstrate how to use the clues to build a reasoned justification predicting Auntie Em was Medusa. Invite a volunteer to do the same for Mr D.

- Organise the children into small groups. Allow 10 to 20 minutes for them to skim Chapters 1 to 8 and to record any clues that identify Poseidon as Percy's father on photocopiable page 31 'Clues and predictions'. Then bring the class together to share the clues. Ask the children to write a paragraph using their clues beginning: 'I predicted Poseidon was Percy's father because, first,...'

Differentiation

Support: Give the children one or two clues to start them off. For example, Percy's mother loves the sea; she met Percy's father at the beach.
Extension: Invite children to skim the first four chapters for clues that Percy is a demigod.

7. Being Percy

Objective

To draw inferences about characters.

What you need

Copies of *Percy Jackson and the Lightning Thief*, printable pages 'About Percy' and 'About Percy – teacher's version'

What to do

- Ask: *How does Percy introduce himself in Chapter 1?* (troubled kid, ADHD, aged 12, attends Yancy Academy) *What other facts do you find out about him in chapter one?* (feels he's had a miserable life; bad things happen to him on field trips; disliked by Mrs Dodds; often in trouble; unable to learn facts and Greek and Roman names – dyslexic) *What does all this indicate about Percy's opinion of himself?* (low self-esteem)

- Ask: *How do you think Percy feels about himself by the end of the book?* (comes to terms with who he is; more confident; new skills; believes he has a place in life) Talk about Percy's relationship with his father. Ask: *How does Percy feel about Poseidon both before and after meeting him?* Encourage reasoned opinions. Ask: *How would you feel towards Poseidon if you were Percy?* Encourage self-reflection and manage sensitive issues in the class. End by inviting children to share questions they would like to ask Percy.

- The children should then complete printable page 'About Percy'. Explain it requires both facts and opinion. (Printable page 'About Percy – teacher's version' includes the factual answers.) Allow children to work in pairs if they wish.

Differentiation

Support: Provide selected information or page numbers to assist children with the sheet.
Extension: Invite children to prepare a short presentation on the question they would most like to ask Percy and how they predict he would answer, giving reasons for their ideas.

8. Settling tabs and fulfilling prophecies

Objective

To explain and discuss their understanding of what they have read by analysing the book's ending.

What you need

Copies of *Percy Jackson and the Lightning Thief*, printable page 'What's next?'.

What to do

- Asking and answering questions helps children to check comprehension and develop ideas. *Percy Jackson and the Lightening Thief* is full of themes, references, wordplay, humour and, above all, clues. A questioning attitude will help them root out hidden clues and meaning.

- Hold an oral question and answer session to check the children's understanding of the book's ending. Ask searching questions, avoiding 'Yes/No' answers. Ask: *How does Percy 'settle his tab'?* (completes his quest and returns Zeus's master bolt) *What does Percy tell Zeus and why?* (about Kronos; he's concerned as he knows Kronos represents evil) *How does Percy settle his personal tab?* (He meets his father and accepts who he is.) *Who 'settled a tab' with Percy?* (Hades returned his mother in exchange for the helm.)

- Ask: *How does the prophecy come true in the final chapter?* (Luke conjures a pit scorpion to kill Percy before escaping.)

- Remind the children that a book in a series is like a chapter: it needs to lure the reader on to the next. Ask: *What suggests this book is part of a series?* (it has loose ends: Luke and Kronos) Hand out printable page 'What's next?'. Ask the children to work in groups to discuss each character and possible roles in a later book.

Differentiation

Support: Children can complete just one additional storyboard note.
Extension: Encourage children to draw up a plot outline for a new book in the series.

Clue log

● Each time you notice a clue as you read the book, complete the log with the clue, page number and your prediction. Tick any correct predictions as you find out.

Clue	Page	Prediction	✓✗

Percy's heroic journey

● Read the summary for each stage in Percy's journey. Then fill in the chapters from the book that match each stage, including reasons to explain your choices.

Summary of stage	Chapters	My reasons
Ordinary world: hero's ordinary life		
Call: something happens to start the adventure		
Refusal: hero briefly refuses to be drawn in		
Supernatural aid: hero finds a mentor or helper to train or advise him		
Crossing threshold: hero enters other world of unknown rules and values		
Tests, allies, enemies: hero is tested – finds his friends and enemies		
Approach: hero and allies prepare for main challenge in other world		
Ordeal: hero confronts death or greatest fears		
Reward: hero finds what he seeks		
Journey home: hero faces further danger on return to fulfil quest		
Atonement: climax as hero severely tested a final time		
Return: hero completes quest bearing a gift or power to transform		

Clues and predictions

- Find clues in the story that suggest Poseidon is Percy's father. Make notes about them here.

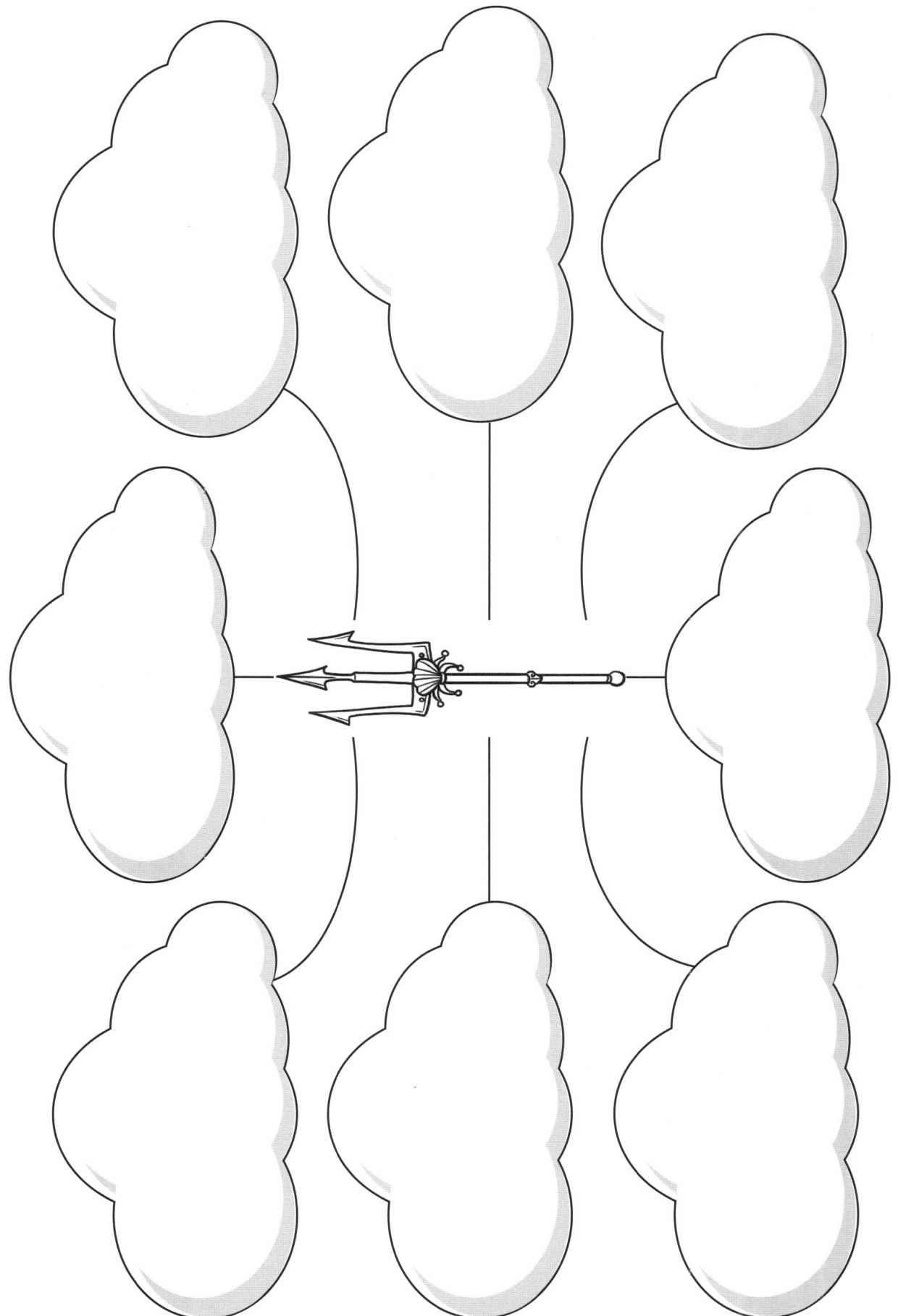

▼ TALK ABOUT IT

1. Are myths just stories?

Objective

To participate in debates.

What you need

Copies of *Percy Jackson and the Lightning Thief*, photocopiable page 35 'It's debatable', timers.

What to do

- When Percy arrives at Camp Half-Blood he thinks myths are just stories that explain nature and what people believed before science. Ask: *How did myths explain natural events and science?* (People didn't always know what they do now; stories helped people understand how things worked.)

- Re-read Chapter 5, highlighting Percy's doubts and what Chiron says to persuade Percy to overcome his doubts. Organise the class into teams to hold a debate on the motion 'The gods from mythology do not exist today'.

- Allow teams time to prepare. Encourage them to start with a brainstorm to establish the main points on both sides (they will need to anticipate the other side's points). They can then divide into sub groups to work on different points. Remind them that, to be convincing, points must be supported by evidence. For example: 'The gods are immortal.' Immortal means 'cannot die', so they must still exist.

- Provide photocopiable page 35 'It's debatable' to clarify how the debate will work. Adapt the guidelines to fit your available time and environment.

Differentiation

Support: Give children slips of paper, each with a statement relating to the debate. They must sort them into 'for' and 'against' piles, to help them understand the different sides to the argument.
Extension: Groups can hold the debate in front of other classes, allowing the audience to choose the winners.

2. Become the Oracle

Objective

To participate in role play.

What you need

Copies of *Percy Jackson and the Lightning Thief*, photocopiable page 36 'A prophecy for Grover', thesauruses, recording device (optional).

Cross-curricular link

History

What to do

- Ask: *Do you think the Oracle in Chapter 9 is based on fact or myth?* (The Oracle was a real priestess in Apollo's temple at Delphi. People consulted her to discover their fate. The problem with her prophecies was their lack of clarity: they could be interpreted differently.)

- Re-read the Oracle section in Chapter 9. Ask: *Which god did Percy think had turned?* (Hades) *Was he right?* (no, it was Ares) *Which parts worried Percy the most?* ('You shall be betrayed by one who calls you friend... And you shall fail to save what matters most, in the end.')

- Ask: *Which verb does the Oracle repeat each time?* ('shall') *What tone does this give the prophecy?* (commanding, forceful, imperious)

- Hand out photocopiable page 36 'A prophecy for Grover' and tell the children that they are going to write the prophecy the Oracle might have given Grover. It should refer to two or three events from the story. Allow time for the children to use a thesaurus to improve word choice and make their prophecies more mysterious.

- Hold a class Oracle consultation to deliver the prophecies and try to decode them. Display the prophecies on the wall. Record them if possible.

Differentiation

Support: Children can write a prophecy in just one sentence.
Extension: Let children also write a prophecy for Annabeth.

3. It's all in the dialogue

Objective

To participate in presentations and performances by making make a trailer to advertise the book.

What you need

Copies of *Percy Jackson and the Lightning Thief*, cinema trailer for the film version of the book (available online), Extracts 2 and 3, recording devices.

What to do

- Start by asking: *What is the difference between narrative and dialogue?* (narrative – recount of events; dialogue – words spoken by characters) *How do you know* how *a character says something – the tone, emphasis and so on?* (verbs, adverbs and context)

- Talk about how trailers advertise films on television or in cinemas. Ask: *Which parts of films are chosen for trailers?* (exciting action, pivotal points, humorous moments and so on) Listen carefully to the audio from the cinema trailer for the film version of the book. Ask for volunteers to imitate the style of the 'voice over' accompanying the trailer; discuss the exaggeration and drama created.

- Hand out copies of Extracts 2 and 3. Organise the class into groups of four. Explain they are going to use the dialogue (Percy, Charon and Hades) to make a trailer with a 'voice-over' advertising the book. Remind them that although a trailer aims to persuade people to watch, it cannot give away the plot. Allow time to practise in class before recording their trailers for other classes to listen to.

Differentiation

Support: Take children aside to listen to them practise their parts, and give advice.
Extension: Encourage groups to use the whole book and include music, props and other effects.

4. Interview the gods

Objective

To participate in role play by interviewing a character.

What you need

Copies of *Percy Jackson and the Lightning Thief*, interactive activity 'Get to know the gods'.

What to do

- Start by asking: *Which Olympian gods are mentioned in the novel?* (Characters: Zeus, Poseidon, Ares, Dionysus – Hades is not strictly an Olympian. Mentioned: Hermes, Aphrodite, Hephaestus, Hera.) Work through the interactive activity 'Get to know the gods' to remind the children about the gods in mythology. Discuss how any modernised versions in the book are different or similar. Ask: *Who narrates the story?* (Percy) *How would the book change if one of the gods were the narrator?* Promote reasoned ideas.

- Tell the children that they are going to role play an interview with one of the 'Big Three' for a teen weekend television show. They will explore the god's opinion of Percy, what happened and whether their opinion of him changed by the end.

- Rather than starting with questions, ask pairs to prepare by thinking of three or four points the god might make about Percy. Once they have their points, the children must formulate questions that would allow the god to make those points. They should make notes (rather than write out their parts) to sound more authentic. Invite volunteers to perform 'live' interviews.

Differentiation

Support: Allow children to work with only two or three points or, to start with the questions.
Extension: The interviewer should add an unexpected question at the end for the god to answer.

5. Family matters

Objective

To participate in discussion about family relationships, linking back to own experience and to ask questions to extend understanding.

What you need

Media resource 'Percy's family tree', interactive activity 'How are you related?'.

What to do

- Hold a quiz on Percy's family. Get the children to write down the names of the following characters as you call them out: Percy's mother, biological father, stepfather, two uncles, grandfather. (Sally Jackson, Poseidon, Gabe Ugliano, Zeus and Hades, Kronos)

- Have a discussion on the concept of 'family': nuclear, extended, historical and so on. Ask: *Does being biologically related to someone automatically make them part of your family?* This is an open question on which the children may have differing views. Manage any sensitive issues relating to family structure.

- Invite children to describe how Percy might feel about his relatives, encouraging empathy with his feelings and comparisons with aspects of their own families.

- Show the media resource 'Percy's family tree'. Ask: *How is Sally related to Zeus?* (his sister-in-law; explain 'in-law' relationships if required) *Does she know or like him?* (know – no; like – unknown.) Invite similar questions from a volunteer before organising the class into small groups to ask each other relationship questions on the gods and goddesses based on the family tree.

Differentiation

Support: Explore the relationships using the interactive activity 'How are you related?'.
Extension: Ask children to add Thalia to the tree and discuss how she is related to everyone. (Zeus's daughter, Percy's first cousin, and so on)

6. Tell me a myth

Objective

To give well-structured narratives by recounting a story.

What you need

Photocopiable page 37 'Myth plotter', recording devices, research resources.

What to do

- Open by asking: *Who can name an Ancient Greek myth?* Make a list on the board. Remind them of the myths linked to the book; for example, 'The Lotus Eaters', 'Perseus and Medusa', 'Persephone in the Underworld'. Invite a volunteer to summarise a myth they remember.

- Tell the children they are going to record a myth of their choice for an audio anthology for other classes to listen to. Ask: *How is listening similar or different from reading a book or watching a film?* (Reading is similar to listening as the reader/listener has to visualise the characters and scenery; films depict the story visually.)

- Allow time to choose and research a myth in books or on the Internet (suggest relevant sites). Hand out photocopiable page 37 'Myth plotter' for children to make notes of the story's key points.

- Ask: *How do you make a story atmospheric to listen to?* (sound effects, expression, different speaking styles for dialogue, dramatic pauses, and so on.) Allow children to work with a partner to help with sound effects and to practise. Let them use any available recording device and set a maximum time limit of three minutes per myth. Compile the audio anthology and hold a myth-telling event for other classes.

Differentiation

Support: Allow children to record using a pre-prepared storyboard.
Extension: Ask children to write and record an introduction for the anthology.

It's debatable

- Use these tips when planning a debate.

A debate is more formal than a discussion. Two people or teams present opposing points of view in a structured way about an issue or assertion. The aim is for each side to convince the audience that their point of view is the right one.

Plan your argument – It doesn't matter if you have to argue a point you disagree with – see it as a challenge.
- Brainstorm reasons that reinforce your point of view.
- Look for evidence (interesting facts or examples to get the audience's attention) to support each point.
- Complete a cue card for each point.
- Practise how you will put each point across.

Present your argument – Stick to an agreed time limit for each speaker and listen to each speaker courteously. Be persuasive by using these techniques:
- persuasive and emotive language
- strong/commanding verbs
- rhetorical or leading questions
- humour
- repetition.

Listen to the opposing arguments – At the end, decide which side is the most convincing or persuasive.

✂

Cue card	**Cue card**
Point	Point
_____	_____
_____	_____
Evidence	Evidence
_____	_____
_____	_____
Persuasive technique	Persuasive technique
_____	_____

A prophecy for Grover

- Use this template to write a prophecy for Grover. Give clues to suggest forthcoming events but remember to retain some mystery.

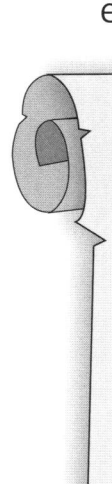

THE ORACLE AT DELPHI

YOU SHALL

YOU SHALL

YOU SHALL

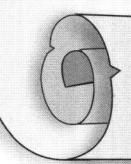

Myth plotter

- Use this storyboard to plot your myth-telling.

Introduction	Setting	Main characters
TIME:	TIME:	TIME:

TIME:	TIME:	TIME:
Problem	Build-up and climax	Resolution and conclusion

Special effects

GET WRITING

1. Compile an encyclopaedia

Objective

To use organisational and presentational devices to structure text and to guide the reader.

What you need

Extract 4, printable page 'Encyclopaedia of Greek gods', photocopiable page 41 'Encyclopaedia entry'.

What to do

- Display Extract 4. Ask: *What type of writing is this?* (non-fiction, reference, information) Discuss the features of non-fiction texts in general: factual, no opinion, third person, mostly past tense, formal language. Ask: *What organisational devices help present information clearly?* (paragraphs, headings, numbering, bold, shading, illustration, columns)

- Tell the children that they are going to design a reference book 'template', in groups, for a class encyclopaedia of ancient gods and goddesses, focusing on an easy-to-use layout that considers what information readers might want.

- Revise how to search for information. Ask: *What helps find information quickly in a reference book?* (contents, index, alphabetical order) *What do you search for?* (key words and phrases) *Is searching on the internet different?* (key words and phrases are still needed but there is more flexibility and choice; the challenge is assessing if it is a reputable source)

- Once their design is approved, they must each select an Ancient Greek god/goddess and complete an encyclopaedia entry about them. Within their groups, encourage them to edit/proofread each other's entries carefully, especially for consistency and correct grammar and spellings.

- Compile and bind their entries into an encyclopaedia using printable page 'Encyclopaedia of Greek Gods' as a cover.

Differentiation

Support: Learners can use photocopiable page 41 'Encyclopaedia entry' as a template.
Extension: Encourage entries incorporating more extensive information.

2. How to I-M

Objective

To use organisational devices to write instructions.

What you need

Interactive activity 'Blueberry smoothie recipe', copies of *Percy Jackson and the Lightning Thief*, photocopiable page 42 'How to I-M', printable page 'Instructions checklist'.

What to do

- Start by giving the children a simple set of instructions. For example: 'Stand up, raise your hands in the air, clap twice, put your hands on your head, sit down.' If anyone takes their hands off their heads while sitting down, point out that you didn't give that instruction.

- Discuss types of instructions: recipe, directions, how to... and so on. Open interactive activity 'Blueberry smoothie recipe'. Sequence the steps together while demonstrating features of instructions: clear outcome, steps in correct order (numbered or bulleted), materials/ingredients, command verbs, clear short sentences, linking words (optional) diagram or picture (optional).

- Re-read Chapter 18 where Annabeth does 'obedience school'. Invite a volunteer to transform how she deals with Cerberus into a set of instructions entitled 'How to train a three-headed dog', using linking words ('first', 'next', and so on).

- Now ask them to write a set of 'How to' instructions for 'I-M'ing (Chapter 15), using photocopiable page 42 'How to I-M' for support if necessary. Encourage pairs to compare instructions, discuss differences and then revise accordingly. Provide printable page 'Instructions checklist' to check their instructions.

Differentiation

Support: Allow children to write instructions using photocopiable page 42 'How to I-M' before copying them into their books.

3. Grover's searcher application

Objective

To select appropriate vocabulary and use organisational devices to write a persuasive letter.

What you need

Copies of *Percy Jackson and the Lightning Thief*, slips of paper, printable page 'Searcher application'.

Cross-curricular link

PSHE

What to do

- Use slips of paper to compile a class profile of Grover. Ask each child to write five things they know about Grover, each on a separate note. Stick them on the board, grouping similar ones. Differentiate between facts and opinions, asking questions to elicit reasons to support children's ideas. Where possible, encourage the children to identify where in the book their ideas come from (for example, Grover is an environmentalist – he hates pollution; beginning of Chapter 12).

- Ask: *What does Grover want to get?* (a searcher's licence) Ask: *Why do you think Pan disappeared?* Prompt an association between Pan disappearing and humans damaging the environment.

- Ask: *How do you think Grover persuaded the Council of Cloven Elders to grant his licence?* (helped Percy on his quest, more mature, more experience, and so on) Discuss persuasive language: clear point of view; reasons with supporting evidence; linking words to build an argument ('however', 'furthermore', and so on); persuasive devices (strong words, gaining agreement, repetition); restating point or request at the end.

- Provide the printable page 'Searcher application' for the children to write Grover's application letter.

Differentiation

Support: Talk through the children's points to help them plan their letters.
Extension: Children can develop their letter into a persuasive speech to give in front of a panel.

4. Add a chapter

Objective

To add an episode by writing a narrative and describing settings, characters, atmosphere and integrating dialogue.

What you need

Copies of *Percy Jackson and the Lightning Thief*, photocopiable page 43 'Chapter planner'.

What to do

- Ask the children to open *Percy Jackson and the Lightning Thief* at the contents page. Ask: *Which chapters describe Percy, Annabeth and Grover's challenges on their journey to the Underworld?* (Chapters 10 to 17) Ask volunteers to summarise the main issue in each chapter. (Note that some chapters, such as 12, don't include a challenge, test or monster.)

- Remind the children that chapters are like short stories – episodes – within the overall story. Organise the class into groups. Ask each group to choose a journey chapter (leave out Chapter 12) to identify its introduction, problem, climax and resolution. Point out that while chapters don't always follow the pattern exactly, each one has a beginning, middle and end.

- Explain that in groups they are going to plan another episode in the trio's journey, using photocopiable page 43 'Chapter planner'. Remind them the new chapter must follow an existing chapter and lead into the next.

- Once their plan is complete, ask the children to develop their ideas independently and to write a chapter summary, introduction and example conversation. Suggest they focus on the characters' styles of speaking, as well as verbs and adverbs to indicate how they speak.

- Let groups share their new chapter ideas.

Differentiation

Support: Allow children to write in pairs rather than individually.
Extension: Ask the children to complete the remainder of the chapter.

GET WRITING

5. Judge the Underworld

Objective

To write a piece of non-fiction based on the plot of the book, selecting appropriate grammar and vocabulary.

What you need

Research resources, A4 paper.

Cross-curricular links

History, PSHE

What to do

- Ask: *According to Percy, who judges the dead when they enter Erebus?* (King Minos, Thomas Jefferson, Shakespeare and similar) Ask: *Why do you think they were chosen as judges?* (famous figures: Minos – first king of Crete; Jefferson – early United States president; Shakespeare – famous English playwright) *Are they real or mythical?* (mythical, real, real)

- Explain that in mythology, Minos was a judge, together with his brother, Rhadamanthus, and Aeacus – all mortal sons of Zeus (like Percy) and considered worthy to judge lives of mortals. In Ancient Greece, they would have been well-known figures. Ask: *What characteristics should someone have to qualify as a judge?* (Remind them that fame alone is not enough.)

- Ask: *Who would you choose to be a judge today?* Take suggestions but guide them to choose from both women and men – the world has changed from Ancient Greek times. Each child must choose one person as a judge and write a brief biography followed by a paragraph giving reasons for their choice. Allow research time and emphasise that this is formal writing that requires correct language and spelling. Let partners proofread each other's drafts before writing them on A4 paper for an 'Updated Underworld Bench' display.

Differentiation

Support: Provide a framework to help children plan their motivation.
Extension: Children can write motivations for three modern judges rather than one.

6. Summarise the story

Objective

To précis the story.

What you need

Copies of *Percy Jackson and the Lightning Thief*, printable page 'Editing guidelines', interactive activity 'Bare essentials'.

What to do

- Ask: *What are the key features of a summary?* (a brief overview, enough to get the gist) Point out that any type of text – sentences, paragraphs, chapters, whole stories, non-fiction texts – can be summarised.

- Ask the children to skim read Chapter 1 and, in pairs, list the key events. Share the lists and demonstrate how to turn the points into a flowing paragraph using linking words (conjunctions, adverbs and prepositions) and present tense verbs.

- Explain they are going to summarise *Percy Jackson and the Lightning Thief*. Use interactive activity 'Bare essentials' to plan the paragraphs as a class to correspond to the different story stages. For example: Percy discovers he's a half-blood; Percy discovers he's Poseidon's son and is offered a quest; Percy, Annabeth and Grover journey to the Underworld; Percy completes his quest; Percy fulfils the prophecy. Demonstrate how to list the stages in the journey paragraph, introduced by a colon, and either with bullets or separated by semi-colons within the paragraph.

- After the planning, set aside a quiet period to allow the children to write their summaries. Hand out printable page 'Editing guidelines' for them to use while editing and revising their work.

Differentiation

Support: Allow children to summarise a chapter rather than the whole story.
Extension: Allow pairs to edit and comment on each other's summaries to improve them, focusing on flow and coherence.

Encyclopaedia entry

- Choose a god or goddess and then search for relevant information to complete this template.
- Edit and proofread your entry in your group.

Name: _____ is the god/goddess

of _____

Appearance

Personality

Attributes/special possessions

Famous myths and adventures

Relatives

How to I-M

- Cut out the steps explaining how to I-M. Paste them onto A4 paper in sequence. Then fill in each space with a suitable connecting word.
- Add a diagram to illustrate the steps.

✂

_____ a rainbow appears, ask the goddess Iris to accept your offering.

_____, find a sunny spot.

_____, throw your payment into the rainbow.

_____, generate a fine mist, using a spray gun or a car wash.

_____, to end the conversation, stop the mist.

_____, start speaking.

_____ payment has been accepted, say the name of the place or person you want to contact.

Diagram

Chapter planner

- Add notes to each part of the planner to help you organise your ideas for a chapter, including a 'Percy-style' title.

Chapter title: _____

Between Chapters: _____ and _____

New characters	Setting for episode

Problem/issue	Build-up/events

Climax	Resolution

▼ ASSESSMENT

1. Underworld A to Z

To participate in role play, giving and listening to directions.

Extract 4, media resource 'The Underworld', printable page 'The Underworld'.

What to do

- Hand out copies of Extract 4 and then read aloud the sections of Chapters 18 and 19 that describe the Underworld and its entrance. Ask the children to note words and phrases related to the Underworld mentioned as you read. Open the media resource 'The Underworld'. Invite volunteers to locate places on the map using compass directions, prepositions and landmarks. For example: 'The Fields of Asphodel are north of the Styx, south of the Plain of Judgment and next to the Vale of Mourning.'

- Encourage pairs to practise by asking one another to locate other places in the Underworld, describing where they are in the same way.

- Hand out the printable page 'The Underworld'. Organise the children into groups to role play giving directions from one Underworld place to another. Demonstrate with a volunteer.

- Each child should start with a partner, then move on to another in the group, taking turns to direct and listen. Assess children's ability to both listen carefully and give polite, clear, sequential directions.

Support: Listen to and give prompts to groups to provide extra guidance.
Extension: Encourage children to give directions from memory rather than using the map. Let their partner check, using the sheet.

2. Then and now

To consider how authors develop characters.

Copies of *Percy Jackson and the Lightning Thief*, printable pages 'Profile cards' and 'Modern makeover'.

What to do

- Ask: *In mythology, Ares is the god of what?* (war) Re-read the description of Ares in Chapter 19. Ask: *What is Ares like?* Look for more reflective suggestions than just 'wicked' or 'evil'. After compiling some words and phrases from the children on the board, ask: *How does the author build up Ares' character and personality?* (what he looks like; his clothes; his bike and knife; his eyes; how he makes Percy feel; the way he speaks and so on) *How does the way Ares looks suit his role as god of war?* (Everything suggests someone aggressive, powerful, violent – not someone to mess with.)

- Explain they are going to describe a modern-day Hermes or Athena. Remind them that while the gods and mythological characters have been modernised in the story, they still reflect their mythological traits and characteristics. For example, in mythology, Ares was violent and war-like, disliked by most of the other gods and often suffered humiliating defeats.

- Ask the children to choose either Hermes or Athena from the printable page 'Profile cards', and hand out copies of printable page 'Modern makeover'. They should complete the character planner for their chosen god as they might appear in a *Percy Jackson* book. Assess how creatively they reflect their modernised god's traditional personality in both the illustration and the written paragraph.

Extension: Children can do a modern profile of both Hermes and Athena.

3. Heroic feats or feet?

Objective

To distinguish between homophones and to use dictionaries to check the meaning of words.

What you need

Interactive activity 'Feet or feat?', dictionaries.

What to do

- Discuss English as a 'survival' language, always borrowing and adapting. Point out how Shakespearian English is quite difficult for a modern English speaker to understand. Ask: *Who can name languages some English words are derived or borrowed from?* (Ancient Greek, Latin, French and so on) Ask: *Why do we specify* Ancient *Greek?* (Modern Greek is different)

- Write 'homophone' and 'homograph' on the board. Draw on their prior knowledge of suffixes, prefixes and etymology by asking: *Which language are these words derived from?* (Ancient Greek) Underline 'homo' to differentiate the two parts of each word. Ask: *What does each word element mean?* ('homo' – same; 'graph' – written; 'phone' – sound) *Do you know other words with similar prefixes/suffixes?* ('telephone', 'phonetic', 'homogenous', and so on)

- Ask: *What's the difference between a homophone and a homograph?* (homophone – words pronounced the same but differing in spelling and meaning; homograph – words spelled the same but differing in meaning and pronunciation) *How can you tell which word is the right one to use?* (context and dictionary)

- Open the interactive activity 'Feet or feat?' and assess the children's ability to use a dictionary and context to select the correct words.

Differentiation

Support: Remind children how to use the dictionary to establish the contextually correct word.
Extension: Encourage children to challenge each other with other homophones or homographs.

4. Comprehension activity

Objective

To understand what they read.

What you need

Copies of *Percy Jackson and the Lightning Thief*, dictionaries, notebooks, printable page 'Questions and answers', interactive activity 'Percy Jackson quiz', printable page 'More questions and answers'.

What to do

- Open by asking: *Who is Percy's father?* (Poseidon) Then ask: *Do you think what Poseidon told Percy is true: that a hero's fate is never happy?* Discuss the children's ideas, encouraging reasoned opinions. Remind them about open and closed questions: closed questions require specific information or a yes/no answer, whereas open questions require opinion and reflection backed by the text.

- Revise general (fiction or non-fiction) comprehension technique: skim read, checking for clues – title, headings, layout, pictures, key words such as names and places, first and last sentences; scan the text, focusing on detail and comprehending unfamiliar words in context; read the questions to identify the type of answer required; re-read the text closely, recording relevant information – highlighting and underlining, if appropriate, or using notepads; write out answers using full sentences where appropriate.

- Ask the children to complete printable page 'Questions and answers', using dictionaries and the book for reference.

- Assess children's ability to work independently, as well as their capacity to recognise and respond to lower and higher order questions.

Differentiation

Support: Let children complete interactive activity 'Percy Jackson quiz', which has multiple choice answers.
Extension: Children can answer the questions on printable page 'More question and answers' in their notebooks.

ASSESSMENT

5. Reviewer's corner

To identify the audience for and purpose of the writing, selecting the appropriate form and models.

Copies of *Percy Jackson and the Lightning Thief*, photocopiable page 47 'Percy Jackson review'.

What to do

- Talk about the book as a whole to promote discussion of its features and themes. Ask: *How did Percy change during the book?* (from low self-esteem, 'troubled kid' to hero half-blood with greater confidence in himself and his skills) Ask: *According to Grover, why did Percy mail Medusa's head to Olympus?* (wanted to make his father take note and be proud) *Do you think Poseidon was proud of Percy? What did he do to show this?* (yes; he returned Medusa's head for Percy to use as he thought best)

- Ask: *Is the book serious or humorous?* (humorous with some serious moments or themes) Encourage a discussion, with children giving examples of when it is one, the other or both at the same time. For example, Percy's early experiences reveal how difficult it can be to feel different or have a difficult home situation, yet he always has a quip and uses humour to manage his emotions and reactions.

- Hand out copies of the photocopiable page 47 'Percy Jackson review' and ask the children to design a review for other children considering reading the book. Assess the children's ability to work with both fact and opinion when writing for a defined audience and purpose.

Support: Talk to the children to help them establish their views and reasons.
Extension: Encourage the children to write a blurb for the back of book as well.

6. Rewrite the myth of Persephone

To write a modern retelling describing settings, characters and atmosphere.

Printable page 'Persephone and Hades', media resource 'Pomegranates', thesauruses.

What to do

- Start by asking: *Has anyone eaten a pomegranate?* If possible, bring one to the class and cut it open to show the jewel-like seeds inside the shrivelled unappealing exterior. Alternatively, display media resource 'Pomegranates' to help the children visualise the tempting, exotic fruit.

- Ask: *Does anyone know the story of Persephone?* If anyone does, ask them to summarise it. Several children may be able to add elements to the story. Hand out copies of printable page 'Persephone and Hades'. Ask the children to read it silently, before asking: *What natural cycle did this myth explain for people in Ancient Greece?* (annual cycle of seasons)

- Re-read excerpts from Chapter 19 describing Hades to remind the children that, although gods are modernised in *Percy Jackson*, they retain their essential characteristics.

- Tell the children they are going to rewrite 'Persephone and Hades' as a modern myth. They should use the printable sheet to highlight key aspects of the story to modernise. Encourage use of a thesaurus when editing. Assess the children's ability to write descriptive narrative to retell a myth with a modern twist.

Support: Provide children with a word bank to enhance their word choices.
Extension: Allow children to read their myths in groups to get suggestions for further enhancement.

Percy Jackson review

- Use this template to complete your review of *Percy Jackson and the Lightning Thief* for other children to read.

Title: _____

Author: _____

Publisher: _____

Genre: _____

First published: _____

Age level: _____

Main characters: _____

Setting: _____
_____

Extract: _____
_____
_____
_____

Plot summary: _____
_____
_____

Themes: _____

I recommend this book for… _____
_____

Star rating: ☆ ☆ ☆ ☆ ☆

SCHOLASTIC

Available in this series:

978-1407-16066-5

978-1407-16053-5

978-1407-16054-2

978-1407-16055-9

978-1407-16056-6

978-1407-16057-3

978-1407-16058-0

978-1407-16059-7

978-1407-16060-3

978-1407-16061-0

978-1407-16062-7

978-1407-16063-4

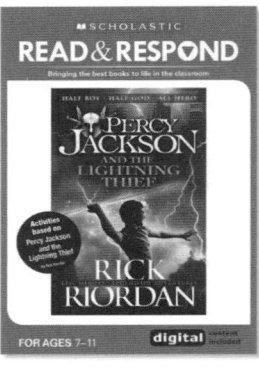
978-1407-16064-1

978-1407-16065-8 **JAN 2017**

978-1407-16052-8 **JAN 2017**

978-1407-16067-2 **JAN 2017**

978-1407-16068-9 **JAN 2017**

978-1407-16069-6 **JAN 2017**

978-1407-16070-2 **JAN 2017**

978-1407-16071-9 **JAN 2017**

To find out more, call: 0845 6039091
or visit our website www.scholastic.co.uk/readandrespond